T0275574

Ross's

Literary Discoveries

Michael Ross

Ross's

Literary Discoveries

Michael Ross

Rare Bird • Los Angeles, Calif.

THIS IS A GENUINE RARE BIRD BOOK

A Rare Bird Book | Rare Bird Books
6044 North Figueroa Street
Los Angeles, CA 90042
rarebirdbooks.com

Set in Minion
Printed in the United States
Distributed worldwide by Publishers Group West

Publisher's Cataloging-in-Publication Data
Names: Ross, Michael, author.
Title: Ross's Literary Discoveries / Michael Ross.
Series: Ross's Quotations.
Description: First Hardcover Edition | A Genuine Rare Bird Book | New York, NY;
Los Angeles, CA: Rare Bird Books, 2023.
Identifiers: ISBN 9781644282434
Subjects: LCSH Communication—Quotations, maxims, etc. | Quotations, English. |
BISAC REFERENCE / Quotations
Classification: LCC PN90 .R67 2019 | DDC 302.2—dc23

*To my parents and all the educators
and authors whose influence led
me to read literary fiction.*

Introduction

W hen I am writing an introduction to a new volume of quotes, I feel like I am highly likely to repeat what I have written in introductions to earlier volumes. Although I am very fond of quotes, I would prefer not to be quoting myself in this endeavor. I have previously described my introduction to literary fiction and my history collecting what I found to be interesting observations by narrators and characters in novels, short stories, and plays.

Even after reading more than 1,400 books, mostly literary fiction, I am still collecting quotes as I read two or three books contemporaneously. Some of these quotes relate to topics included in one or more of the first eight volumes, while others may find their way into new books on topics, such as the arts, mortality, fate, our control of our lives (or lack thereof), law, lawyers, government, justice, and honesty. As my collection grows, I am tempted to offer sequels to earlier volumes that include quotes about, for example, men and women, love, sex, marriage, age, time, past/present/future, and memory.

For quite some time, I have been hoping to accumulate a sufficient number of quotes for this volume. As an avid reader of literary fiction, quotes about books, fiction, novels, and literature are obviously of interest to me. I confess that I deviated from my long-standing practice of not selecting books to read based upon my perception of their likelihood of giving me quotes on certain topics. Most of the books I chose to increase the number of quotes on these topics did yield relevant quotes, and I did not sacrifice the quality of the books I read in the process. I believe that my extensive reading of literary fiction has given me at least some measure of credibility in selecting these quotes and making brief comments about them.

I continue to try to expand the number of authors whose books I read. I have lately referred to *1000 Books to Read Before You Die* for suggestions. I had already read quite a few of the recommended books and, if not the specific books, other books by the recommended authors. Some of these new authors are: Douglas Adams, Giovanni Boccaccio, Ray Bradbury, Daphne du Maurier, Ralph Ellison, Jack Finney, Nicolai Gogol, Patricia Highsmith, Carlo Levi, Alan Paton, Virginia Woolf, Iris Murdoch, Haruki Murakami, and Jean Rhys.

My mission in offering quotes in this volume is not to advocate the truth of their contents because, in part, some are contradictory. More important, my main objective is simply to share with my readers the "nuggets" I have discovered. I also hope to amuse and stimulate readers, and, in some cases, introduce them to new books and authors.

Books

Literary fiction contains numerous commentaries about books. Most are positive, but a few are neutral or downright negative, the last of which may be surprising coming from authors of books. Let us start with a few negative comments and some neutral ones before concentrating on the accolades for books.

The first quote is short but not sweet.

«◇»

"What do we want with books anyway? There are too many books already...."

Henry Miller, Tropic of Cancer

Here is a much more fulsome complaint, with an unusual metaphor and detailed description of the fate of many books, but not the ones I have read.

«»

"Anyway, I decided, if there was anything the human race had a sufficiency of, a sufficiency and a surfeit, it was books. When I thought of the cataracts of books, the Niagras of books, the rushing rivers of books, the tons of truckloads and trainloads of books that were pouring off the presses of the world at the moment, only a very few of which would be worth picking up and looking at, let alone reading, I began to feel that it was admirable that he hadn't written it. One less book to clutter up the world, one

less book to take up space and catch dust and go unread from bookstores to homes to second-hand bookstores and junk stores and thrift shops to still other homes to still other second-hand bookstores and junk stores and thrift shops to still other homes ad infinitum."

Joseph Mitchell, "Joe Gould's Secret" in
Up in the Old Hotel

I wonder if "everything" includes even the plight of books described above.

«◊»

"...But jackets are the redheaded stepchildren of book publishing. We blame them for everything."

Gabrielle Zevin, The Storied Life of A. J. Fikry

The author is referring to
Pride and Prejudice.

«»

"You have to have some life under your belt before you can make any sense of a book like that."

Tobias Wolff, "Sanity" in *The Night in Question*

This speculation may be slightly veiled
praise for books.

«»

*Books are not life, however much we might
prefer it if they were.*

𝒥𝓊𝓁𝒾𝒶𝓃 ℬ𝒶𝓇𝓃ℯ𝓈, *Flaubert's Parrot*

It is difficult to argue with this generalization, but I think many readers have reread favorite books and gotten quite a bit from the effort.

«»

...the things we respond to at twenty are not necessarily the same things we will respond to at forty and vice versa. This is true in books and also in life.

Gabrielle Zevin, *The Storied Life of A. J. Fikry*

I like this metaphor for a book, which lauds books' immense powers.

«»

I thought again what an achievement a book is, a magic box simultaneously holding the presence of the author and the wonders of the world.

Ivan Doig, Sweet Thunder

This may be true for the narrator,
an author who has had only one
book published.

«◊»

"*After all, the author is the book and the
book is the author.*"

Jason Mott, Hell of a Book

Here is an observation that rings true, but some books intentionally or accidentally leave some things to our imagination.

«»

Books are where things are explained to you; life is where things aren't.

Julian Barnes, Flaubert's Parrot

This seems to me to be a bit of an
exaggeration, especially if the memory
is a pleasant one.

«◊»

*His editor further argued that only in a
book is a man willing to live forever with
a memory.*

ℒℯℴ𝓃 𝒰𝓇𝒾𝓈, *The Angry Hills*

The context for this quote is the
character's praise of books, presumably
well-written ones.

«»

*"Every word the right one and exactly where
it should be. That's basically the highest
compliment I can give."*

Gabrielle Zevin, *The Storied Life
of A. J. Fikry*

It is interesting how we discover books that are relevant for us, even when we do not expect it.

«»

Once, she would never have even opened a book by an older person: nothing to do with her, she would have felt. But what could be odder than the way that books which chime with one's condition or stage in life insinuate themselves into one's hand?

Doris Lessing, love, again

The author may be biased, but his comparison seems apt. It does, however, make me wonder about the quality of the films he watches.

«◊»

Escaping into a film is not like escaping into a book. Books force you to give something back to them, to exercise your intelligence and imagination, whereas you can watch a film—and even enjoy it—in a state of mindless passivity.

Paul Auster, A Man in the Dark

High praise, indeed, from the late author
of very successful and well-written novels
set in the West.

«◊»

*What a wealth we are granted, in the books
that carry the best in us through time.*

Ivan Doig, Sweet Thunder

This expression of admiration for the positive effects of books may seem a little old-fashioned, but it comes across as very heartfelt.

《》

At the time of their invention, books were devices as crassly practical for storing or transmitting language, albeit fabricated from scarcely modified substances found in forest and field and animals, as the latest Silicon Valley miracles. But by accident, not by cunning calculation, books, because of their weight and texture, and because of their sweetly token restrictions to manipulation, involve our hands and eyes, and then our minds and souls, in a spiritual adventure I would be very sorry for my grandchildren not to know about.

Kurt Vonnegut, Timequake

I began reading novels by this author relatively late but find his descriptions, like this one, very engaging, especially the personification of books.

«»

Fortunately, there are books. We can leave them on a shelf or in a trunk, abandon them to the dust and moths, dump them in dark cellars, we may not even lay eyes on them or touch them for years and years, but they don't mind, they wait quietly, closed in upon themselves so that none of their contents are lost, for the moment that always arrives, the day when we ask ourselves, I wonder where that book…has got to, and the book, summoned at last, appears.

José Saramago, *The Cave*

Hyperbole or not, this is a succinct and
powerful testament.

《》

"There is no glory greater than a book...."
𝒞𝒶𝓇𝓁ℴ𝓈 ℱ𝓊ℯ𝓃𝓉ℯ𝓈, *The Campaign*

Readers

Books would not be of much interest without readers, or, these days, listeners. However they are experienced, they are, at least, part of the reason for which writers write. They are us, the audience, if you will. Most of the commentary about readers I have discovered is at least neutral and more often positive.

This quote suggests writers should not have to edit their work to eliminate some of life's breadth.

«»

We think that Life's performance is too sweeping, too uneven, that her genius is too untidy. To indulge our readers we cut out of Life's untrammeled novels our neat little tales for the use of schoolchildren.

Vladimir Nabokov, "The Passenger" in *Details of a Sunset*

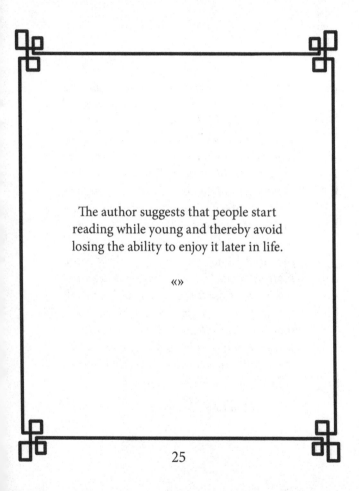

The author suggests that people start reading while young and thereby avoid losing the ability to enjoy it later in life.

《》

Men and women say that they will read, and think so,—those I mean, who have acquired no habit of reading,—believing the work to be, of all works, the easiest. It may be work, they think, but of all works it must be easiest of achievement. Given the absolute faculty of reading, the task of going through the pages of a book must be, of all tasks, the most certainly within the grasp of the man or woman who attempts it! Alas, no;—if the habit be not there, of all tasks it is the most difficult. If a man have not acquired the habit of reading till he is old, he shall sooner in his old age learn to make shoes than learn the adequate use of a book. And worse again;—under such circumstances the making of shoes shall be more pleasant to him than the reading of a book.

Anthony Trollope, The Claverings

This is a curious assertion that makes
me wonder if the character had much
evidence to support it.

«»

*...he always said that women were the most
enthusiastic readers of fiction, not men.*

John Irving, *Avenue of Mysteries*

The dichotomy may be true, but how will we ever know?

«»

Great publishers were not always great readers, and good readers seldom made good publishers....

James Salter, All That Is

This is an interesting observation about reading's relationship to the principal female character who is charting her way toward death at a relatively young age.

«»

Because reading presupposed a future. It had to do with fortification.

Martin Amis, *London Fields*

Here is a quote from the author's fictional
tale of Henry James' life and work.

«»

*Reading was as silent and solitary and
private as writing.*

Colm Tóibín, *The Master*

For this character, reading provided a much sought after peace of mind.

«»

She had begun to read in the beginning as a protection from the frightening and unpleasant things. She continued because, apart from the story, literature brought with it a kind of gentility for which she craved.

Patrick White, The Tree of Man

Here is a prescription for maintaining our sanity.

«»

The thing is you have to read books or you'll drive yourself up the wall.

Jim Harrison, Sundog

She bemoans the decline of reading and, as a result "great" readers. The mirror metaphor is interesting but subject to debate.

«»

Bea says that the art of reading is slowly dying, that it's an intimate ritual, that a book is a mirror that offers us only what we already carry inside us, that when we read, we do it with all our heart and mind, and great readers are becoming more scarce by the day.

Carlos Ruiz Zafón, *The Shadow of the Wind*

Another female character finds solace in
the novels she reads.

《》

*She must have been tired by the of other
voices, save those she discovered in novels
where a plot might swerve wildly and then
somehow turn easily for home during the
last two or three chapters.*

Michael Ondaatje, Warlight

The metaphor in this quote offers an excellent idea of how reading, if done well, can transport us.

«»

"You can learn almost everything from reading…The same method doesn't work for everyone, each person has to invent his or her own, whichever suits them best, some people spend their entire lives reading but never get beyond reading the words on the page, they don't understand that the words are merely stepping stones placed across a fast-flowing river, and the reason they're there is so that we can reach the farther shore, it's the other side that matters…"

José Saramago, The Cave

It seems unnecessary to say much
about this famously erudite author's
proclamation, which I trust the author has
correctly attributed.

《》

Only reading counts; Nabokov said.
　　　Michael Ondaatje, Divisadero

Writers

Some commentary on writers has been unfavorable while others have explained how difficult their tasks and lives are. Some of the quotes below are merely descriptive, without obvious negative or positive judgment. There are, of course, some accolades and glowing expressions of appreciation for authors. We will explore examples of each.

We start with a nonjudgmental
observation about why writers write.

《》

But after all every writer writes because it's
his mode of living.

F. Scott Fitzgerald, *The Beautiful and*
Damned

This seems like a very damning generalization, and I could not bear to think of my favorite authors this way.

«»

"For many happy years I've listened to writers and their brilliant kvetching…The most successful writers make the biggest complainers….I wonder if the qualities that produce a top writer also account for the ingenuity and size of his complaints. Does writing come out of bitterness and rage or does it produce bitterness and rage?"

Don DeLillo, Mao II

I wonder about this harsh indictment
of writers; perhaps it applies to some
of the author's competitors, not the
author himself.

«◇»

*Writers by experience are over-trained in
cynicism, and cynicism along with irony is
a device, a set of blinders, to keep the world
in its place. Writers pretty much think they
are what the total consensus of opinion says
they are.*

Jim Harrison, Sundog

Could this very brief exclamation be
anything more than hyperbole?

«»

What lunatics writers are...
Elizabeth Goudge, The Scent of Water

Writers may well be entertainers, as many artists are, but do they deserve the scatological last line?

《》

A writer has no responsibilities, for responsibilities are the burden of power. He is, at best, an entertainer, like that trained bear we saw nodding its head and catching apples in its mouth the other evening. At less than best, he is an oaf who lets farts at both ends.

John Hersey, The Conspiracy

Here is an interesting question that seems
to imply that writers' private thoughts
may be shocking.

《》

*What would normal people think if they
knew what went on in a writer's mind below
the surface?*

Elizabeth Goudge, The Scent of Water

If all writers fit this description, how would they know enough about life to write convincingly about it?

«»

What did writers do with their time? They were the most unadventurous souls on earth, weren't they? Sitting all day at their desks.

Graham Swift, Mothering Sunday: A Romance

At least this author gives writers a little, begrudging credit for observing life.

«»

...telling us no more than that Proust liked to watch others in the act of love through a hole in the wall, a nice symbol since writers are essentially voyeurs, reporting what they have glimpsed out of the eye's corner or overheard at another table, meditating continually upon what others do.

Gore Vidal, *Two Sisters*

Not having met any of my favorite authors, I cannot vouch for the accuracy of this quote.

《》

Meeting one of your favorite authors in the world can be scary. It's so easy to be let down.

Madeleine L'Engle, A House Like a Lotus

This is an explanation offered for why writers' women commit suicide.

«»

...writers are nightmares. Writers are nightmares from which you cannot awake. Most alive when alone, they make living hard to do for those around them.

Martin Amis, The Information

Here is another gripe about writers' lack
of sufficient life experience.

«»

*"Writing is one thing, but experiencing life
is more important."*

Cristina Henriquez, "Mercury" in *Come
Together, Fall Apart*

Is writing alone the cause of the
unfortunate lives that some authors
have lead?

«◊»

*"Think of all the lost writers who wrote
beautifully and lived miserably."*

Ray Bradbury, "The F. Scott/Tolstoy/
Ahab Accumulator" in *One More for the
Road*

This contemporary author probably does not include himself among those he chastises for their failure to keep up with the times.

«»

Perhaps because of their addiction to form, writers always lag behind the contemporary formlessness. They want to write about an old reality, in a language that's even older. It's not the words: it's the rhythms of thought. In this sense all novels are historical novels.

Martin Amis, *London Fields*

I suppose that because writing is usually a solitary endeavor, it allows for a fair dose of mischief.

«»

"He was a writer. A writer. They have time to get into trouble."

Michael Ondaatje, *Anil's Ghost*

Here is a somewhat ironic observation about the relationship between the writer and his or her reader.

«»

...the writer wrote alone, and the reader read alone, and they were alone together.

A. S. Byatt, Possession: A Romance

I cannot verify that Thoreau said this, but
I like the humor in any case.

《》

*Thoreau said a writer was a man with
nothing to do who finds something to do.*

Richard Ford, The Lay of the Land

This famous, prolific author identifies
a risk writers face, but is it so different
from the risk faced by anyone working on
a long project? He uses some humorous
suggestions about risks to be avoided.

«»

Any author who has undertaken a lengthy enterprise must wonder if he or she will see the end of it. If he has sense, he will put himself out of the way of danger for the work's sake, refusing to swim lest he be caught by cramps and drown, avoiding tavern brawls and shell fish. But death, somewhat like God, is a great joker and can lurk in a speck of dirt or the table's edge. The unwary author, safe in his writing cell, chokes on the stone of the plum he sucks for refreshment or finds that life, suddenly grown bored with the monitoring of the drum of his heart, leaves him as he stands to stretch.

Anthony Burgess, The Kingdom of the
Wicked

I wonder if many writers would agree with this ironic quote.

《》

...certainly a life of writing books is a trying adventure in which you cannot find out where you are unless you lose your way.

Philip Roth, The Counterlife

This character's experience may be common, but there are many writers whose early works are far more successful than their later works. I will resist the temptation name any of them.

《》

Morrison's rise was typical of a writer's story of many years of struggle for acceptance, bitter disappointments and the rest of the frustration and tears that plague that supposedly charmed profession.

Leon Uris, The Angry Hills

Is writing such a lonely profession as this
metaphor claims?

«◊»

*Writers—all writers—need to belong. Only
for real writers, unfortunately, their club is
a club with just one member.*

Richard Ford, *The Sportswriter*

Is this a reflection of the most challenging
struggle in writing fiction?

«»

*...it takes only a modest talent to write about
misery—and misery is a more congenial
subject than happiness. Most of us have
known some suffering and can understand
and respond by filling in the gaps. But great
happiness is almost incomprehensible, and
conveying it in print requires genius.*

Paul Theroux, *Hotel Honolulu*

I like this picturesque simile for the novelists' uncertainty about success.

«»

"Writing novels is like putting messages into bottle after bottle and tossing them into the sea on the outgoing tide without any idea of where they'll be washed up or how they will be interpreted."

David Lodge, Home Truths

The simile in this quote makes the author's point quite vividly and efficiently.

«»

The fact that a writer needed solitude didn't mean he was cut off or selfish. A writer was like a monk in his cell praying for the world—something he performed alone, but for other people.

Tobias Wolff, Old School

It seems unfair to blame novelists for the state of the publishing industry and the markets it serves.

《》

The novelist is a capitalist of the imagination. He or she invents a product which consumers didn't know they wanted until it was made available, manufactures it with the assistance of purveyors of risk capital known as publishers, and sells it in competition with makers of marginally differentiated products of the same kind.

David Lodge, *Nice Work*

This makes writers' work sound free-flowing, but more often I have read of how they often struggle with their craft.

«»

...but you know how it is with writing, one word often brings along another in its train simply because they sound good together, even if this means sacrificing respect for levity and ethics for aesthetics...

José Saramago, *The Elephant's Journey*

Here a counterpoint to the quote above, a depiction of the challenging nature of the novelist's work.

«»

I played a mild hunch. That's what writing is, a hundred hunches, a hundred affronts to your confidence, a hundred decisions, every page.

Martin Amis, London Fields

This quote offers a descriptive metaphor
for the solitude involved in writing.

«»

*The only flaw I've ever found with writing
is that you can call out to it, but the page
never answers you back. Writing is an act of
obsession after all.*

Jason Mott, *Hell of a Book*

This quote does not describe the sort of trouble writing brings with it, but it is, nevertheless, quite a warning for aspiring authors.

«»

It seems to me that writing brings trouble with it, more trouble, unexamined trouble. Even to the best.

Martin Amis, *London Fields*

Once again, we have the complaint that writers are captive to the whims of the public's tastes.

«»

One can live by writing these days, if one does it practically all the time and is prepared to write anything the market asks for.

Iris Murdoch, Under the Net

Here is another writer's complaint, this time about the measure of writers' success.

《》

The modern author is only as important as their search results.

Jason Mott, Hell of a Book

What a mixture of metaphors and a simile
to describe the writer's plight!

《》

*For a writer there is no such thing as an
exemplary life. It's a fact that certain writers
do good work at the bottom of a bottle.
The outlaws generally write as well as the
bankers, though more briefly. Some writers
flourish like opportunistic weeds by hiding
among the citizens, others by toughing it out
in one sort of desert or another.*

Tobias Wolff, Old School

This quote uses a very descriptive
metaphor of a sensory experience to
describe what it is like for the author to
begin his or her novel.

«»

Starting a novel is opening a door on a
misty landscape; you can see very little,
but you can smell the earth and feel the
wind blowing.

Iris Murdoch, *Under the Net*

Here is a simile and metaphor for how
a writer may feel upon finishing his or
her work.

«◇»

*Many writers feel this way after completing
an ambitious work; it is like a little death,
one wants to crawl back into some wet
womb and become an egg.*

William Saroyan, Sophie's Choice

Is it simply fate or some inborn trait that
makes one a writer?

《》

*"Writing chooses us," I once told a fan at a
book signing. "All we can do is heed the call."*

Jason Mott, *Hell of a Book*

This seems like very good advice, but I suspect many writers hope to accomplish more than the duty ascribed here.

«◊»

A writer cannot change the world; his duty is to describe it.

John Hersey, *The Conspiracy*

I wonder if "complicated" is the most accurate word here; "interesting" might serve better.

«»

I suppose it comes of being a novelist, that one always prefers a complicated explanation to a simple one.

David Lodge, Thinks...

At first reading this seems provocative,
but is it a distinction without a difference?

«»

Writers are innocent. Not guiltless—just innocent.

Martin Amis, *The Information*

Does this mean that writers, as a group,
are above or below other members
of society?

«»

*Writers formed a society of their own
outside the common hierarchy.*

Tobias Wolff, Old School

Here is an interesting quote, but it does not say if the writer is better or worse off.

«»

So that between the man writing a diary and the traveler there was already a gap, already a gap between the man and the writer.

V. S. Naipaul, The Enigma of Arrival

Compared to practitioners of other crafts
or professions, the writer's work can be
measured only when read.

«»

The skill of writing offers little to a viewer.
Michael Ondaatje, Divisadero

This quote sets a very high standard
for writers.

《》

*Life, it has been agreed by everyone whose
opinion is worth consulting, is the only fit
subject for novelist or biographer;…"*

Virginia Woolf, *Orlando*

Do we think this statement might be true of all or most writers, or only those like Henry James, the subject of this novel?

«»

...each book he had written, each scene described or character created, had become an aspect of him, had entered into his driven spirit and lay there much as the years themselves had done.

Colm Tóibín, *The Master*

Is this the simple recipe for writers'
success, and, if it is, how easy is it
to follow?

«»

*It was the whole point of being a writer,
wasn't it, to embrace the stuff of life? It was
the whole point of life to embrace it.*

Graham Swift, *Mothering Sunday*

In case you wondered what makes writers happy, here is one author's answer.

«»

Writers are happiest with an idea which can become all emotion, and an emotion all idea.

Thomas Mann, *Death in Venice*

One of the most highly regarded
novelists sets a high bar for novelists to
achieve merit.

«»

*A novelist says this and that of his
personages, and if only he knows how
to say it earnestly enough he may not be
questioned upon the inventions of his brain
in which his own belief is made sufficiently
manifest by a telling phrase, a poetic image,
the accent of emotion. Art is great!*

Joseph Conrad, *Under Western Eyes*

Here is a "clarion" call for writers to write!

«»

"Why not write, then,...There is music in words, and it can be heard you know, by thinking."

E. L. Doctorow, Homer & Langley

The author is comparing writers of fiction
to writers of history, whose efforts may
be selective and discriminatory, but is the
final word fair?

«»

*…it is better to be a novelist, a fiction writer,
a liar.*

José Saramago, *The Elephant's Journey*

This quote probably accurately describes
the required skill and devotion of a
successful writer.

«»

*The highest form of writing is of course a
book of one's own, something that has to be
prepared with tact, subtlety, and cunning,
and sustained over many months, like
an affair.*

David Lodge, *Small World*

I may have taken for granted the nature of
the novelist's mission.

«◊»

*But the fellow talked like a cheap novelist.—
Or like a very good novelist for the matter of
that, if it's the business of a novelist to make
you see things clearly.*

Ford Madox Ford, The Good Soldier

Here is some high praise, along with some lofty standards, for novelists.

«»

...writing novels was surely the best thing a person could do in life, for Dostoyevsky had taught him that made-up stories could go far beyond mere fun and diversion, they could turn you inside out and take off the top of your head, they could scald you and freeze you and strip you naked and thrust you out into the blasting winds of the universe,...

Paul Auster, 4 3 2 1

Literature

The term, literature, encompasses a wide variety of written, and these days recorded, works. Some works may be biography, memoirs or autobiography, history, or other non-fiction. A great portion of my reading over the past fifty years or more has been literary fiction, mostly novels and some short stories. I have organized the quotes in this section into three parts—fiction, novels, and literature—because not all fiction and novels are deemed worthy of the label "literature."

Fiction

Is too much fiction published, or is it that much of what is published is not worth reading? In either case, if this is true, who is to blame? The ending similes are creative.

«»

...it made me think about the prolific production of fiction in our culture. Is it over-production? Are we in danger of accumulating a fiction-mountain—an immense quantity of surplus novels, like the butter mountains and milk lakes of the EEC?

David Lodge, *Thinks...*

I prefer to think of quality fiction as more of the former than the latter.

«»

...fiction can be an epistle to the living, but more often the things we write, believing they matter, are letters to the dead.

Paul Theroux, Hotel Honolulu

The character in this story has an aversion
to fiction that does not tackle
important issues.

«»

*He didn't like modern fiction, its narcissism,
it moral timidity, its silence in the face of
great wrongs.*

Tobias Wolff, "The Life of the Body" in
The Night in Question

Although this may be true of some fiction,
I find this an unusual criticism of the
genre in general.

«◇»

*Fiction is so often fatal; it hallows some
places and it makes them look like
dreamland.*

Paul Theroux, The Consul's File

The thrust of this observation is that
works of fiction should be judged only on
their merits not in connection with some
facts or opinions about the author.

«»

*It has literally become impossible for anyone
to read a work of fiction except in terms of the
author's life. Since they have learned to read
at all, the "lives' of artists, the experiences
of artists, the opinions of artists, have been
offered side by side with the works of artists,
which has become infinitely less important.
Plays, novels, stories, poems, are "taught" in
schools, in terms of the author's lives.*

Doris Lessing, The Four-Gated City

This assertion seems an exaggeration at best. Do we all have lives that cannot be fairly reflected in fiction?

«»

We lead lives that even the best fiction can't begin to suggest.

Paul Theroux, The Consul's File

The author of this novel describes Henry James's commitment to writing fiction after his play had flopped.

«»

...he would devote himself, as he had pledged, to the silent art of fiction.

Colm Tóibín, *The Master*

Here is an observation that stories may have some merit in a metaphysical sense.

«»

Stories have no beginning or end; they are continuous and ragged.

Paul Theroux, *The Consul's File*

Readers may judge for themselves if this is broadly true or merely reflects upon the character's life and fiction he reads.

«»

"There is usually more sex in fiction than in life,…"

$\mathcal{D}avid\ \mathcal{L}odge$, Home Truths

Yes, there is, in the best fiction, a great
deal of truth.

«»

*Truth is not a saga of alarming episodes;
it is a detail, a small clear one, that gives
fiction life.*

Paul Theroux, *The Consul's File*

This quote expresses an observation very similar to one of the previous quotes.

«»

It looked as if life were too many-sided to be pinned down to any however realistic novel.

A. A. Milne, *Four Days' Wonder*

I find this generalization at least
overboard if not worse.

«»

*The modern novel should be largely a work
of reference. Most authors spend their time
saying what has been said before—usually
said much better.*

Flann O'Brien, At Swim-Two-Birds

Readers, prepare yourselves for a very unusual metaphor describing how some of you are taking risks by reading novels.

《》

But novels commenced with hesitation or chaos. Readers were never fully in balance. A door a lock a weir opened and they rushed through, one hand holding a gunnel, the other a hat.

Michael Ondaatje, The English Patient

From the same book and author comes some interesting advice that the author himself followed.

«»

The successful defusing of a bomb ended novels.

𝓜𝓲𝓬𝓱𝓪𝓮𝓵 𝓞𝓷𝓭𝓪𝓪𝓽𝓳𝓮, The English Patient

Although this quote harks back to other comparisons between fiction and life, this one is more positive than those.

«»

Real life is too sloppy a model for good fiction,…The good characters in novels are more fully formed than most of the people we know in our lives,…Characters in novels are more understandable, more consistent, more predictable. No good novel is a mess; many so-called real lives are messy.

John Irving, *Avenue of Mysteries*

I like this succinct metaphor for the connection between life and novels.

《》

A novel is a mirror walking down a road.
Michael Ondaatje, The English Patient

Although this observation may be true, it seems a little "tongue in cheek."

«»

Of course, in a novel, peoples' hearts break, and they die, and that is the end of it; and in a story this is very convenient.

Harriet Beecher Stowe, Uncle Tom's Cabin

Here is a wonderful exposition of the potential timelessness of novels.

«»

The novel lives each time it is read. The novel has the past of its dead readers, the present of its living readers, and the future of its readers to come.

Carlos Fuentes, "Constancia" in *Constancia and Other Stories for Virgins*

I wonder if this is truly a limiting factor
for readers' appreciation of literature.

«»

*...who can understand literature unless he
has suffered?*

Thornton Wilder, *The Cabala*

Here a bit of the author's hyperbole about the incidence of adultery in life and fiction.

«»

There were, of course, plenty of unfaithful husbands in literature: modern fiction, in particular, might be described as a compendium of advice on the conduct of adultery.

David Lodge, *The British Museum Is Falling Down*

After all the quotes about fiction's relationship with life, should literature be blamed for its connections with life?

«»

It was the nature of literature to behave like the fallen world it contemplated, this dusky ground where subterfuge reigns and certainty is folly.

Tobias Wolff, *Old School*

Although I have enjoyed a number of this author's novels, I cannot agree with much of this quote.

«»

Life was transparent, literature opaque. Life was open, literature a closed system. Life was comprised of things, literature of words. Life was what it appeared to be about....Literature was never about what it appeared to be about.

David Lodge, *Changing Places*

This comes from the same book and
character as the prior quote about sex in
life and fiction.

«◇»

*"Literature is mostly about having sex and
not much about having children. Life is the
other way round."*

David Lodge, The British Museum Is
Falling Down

A character in this novel chastises a doctor for reading more literature than is good for him.

«»

"Literature, literature…It's been the ruin of many a good surgeon."

Thomas Wolfe, *Look Homeward, Angel*

The author, or at least her character, seems
to feel too limited by history.

«»

*But nothing is more paralyzing than a
sense of historical perspective, especially in
literary matters.*

Iris Murdoch, Under the Net

I suspect that for most of my readers, their relationship with literature is intentional.

«»

We all have our connections with literature, wittingly or not so wittingly.

Martin Amis, The Information

I place works of literary fiction in
this category.

«◇»

*Make no mistake, he said: A true piece of
writing is a dangerous thing. It can change
your life.*

Tobias Wolff, *Old School*

This is certainly a high calling for
literature, one that the author took
very seriously.

«»

*For literature was nothing other than the
union of humanism and politics...*

𝒯homas 𝓜ann, *The Magic Mountain*

Here is another expression of the role of literature in society.

«»

"And if literature is not the Bride and Bedfellow of Truth, what is she?"

Virgina Woolf, *Orlando*

I like the humor in this character's
metaphor and hope you will excuse
the profanity.

«◇»

*"The world must be all fucked up," he said
then, "when men travel first class and
literature goes freight."*

𝒢𝒶𝒷𝓇𝒾𝑒𝓁 𝒢𝒶𝓇𝒸í𝒶 𝑀á𝓇𝓆𝓊𝑒𝓏, One Hundred
Years of Solitude

Here is some high praise for the benefit
of reading literature that relies upon
ancient revelations.

«»

*"Yes, books! Cicero and Ovid have told us
that to literature only could they look for
consolation in their banishment."*

Anthony Trollope, *The Duke's Children*

The context here is contrasting literature
to the main character's journalistic attacks
on public figures.

«»

*...in literature you commemorate people's
experience, their living, and their pain; you
celebrate their humanity.*

Elia Kazan, *The Arrangement*

This quote addresses an alleged contrast
between the best literature and the
"simple moral tales about simple moral
people, light, slight, and tenderly trivial"
allegedly like Hawthorne's tales.

«»

*...had agreed that literature at its most
valuable and rich and intense was written
in the countries which Napoleon had
reigned over and attacked; literature lay
in the places where Roman coins could be
found in the soil.*

Colm Tóibín, *The Master*

People often seek a definition of what constitutes a "classic" in literature, and here is one author's proposed definition.

«»

"A classic...is a successful book that has survived the reaction of the next period or generation. Then it's safe, like a style of architecture or furniture. It's acquired a picturesque dignity to take the place of its fashion...."

F. Scott Fitzgerald, The Beautiful and Damned

Here is a quote with effective and efficient figures of speech to conclude our praise of literature.

«»

"Literature, at least good literature, is science tempered with the blood of art. Like architecture or music."

Carlos Ruiz Zafón, The Angel's Game

Conclusion

I have often been asked to identify my favorite books and authors of literary fiction. Without having looked back at these volumes, I believe that many are the sources of the quotes I have offered in these volumes.

Although I sometimes wonder if I should have read, or should be reading, more biographies, histories, and other non-fiction, I tend to stick with literary fiction. It may be inertia or laziness because it is what I know best. I have spent very little time reading science fiction, fantasy, and pulp fiction. Lately, I have been focusing on classics, prize-winning authors, and books, as well as those recommended by reliable sources. In any case, I hope I have done some justice to books, fiction, novels, and literature, for which I have offered quotes in this volume.

I would like to express my deep appreciation for Tyson Cornell's enthusiastic support and creative ideas for this third volume of my quotations, and for the hard work by all of the staff at Rare Bird, including Alice Marsh-Elmer for the development and execution of the excellent design, inside and out, of the book; Hailie Johnson; Guy Intoci; and Alexandra Watts.

Thanks to Cara Lowe for the illustrations.

Visit michaelrossauthor.com